Tongues?

by

KENNETH E. HAGIN

PART I

THE BIBLE WAY TO RECEIVE THE HOLY SPIRIT

The infilling of the New Testament believers with the Holy Ghost should be our pattern today. I propose that we look at the Acts of the Apostles, see how they did it, and follow their example in getting people filled with the Holy Ghost.

In the first chapter of Acts, just before Jesus ascended on high, we see this great scene:

ACTS 1:4-5

4 And, being assembled together with
them, (Jesus) commanded them that they
should not depart from Jerusalem, but wait
for the promise of the Father, which, saith
he, ye have heard of me.

5 For John truly baptized with water;
but ye shall be baptized with the Holy
Ghost not many days hence.

And then on the day of Pentecost:

ACTS 2:1-4

1 And when the day of Pentecost was
fully come, they were all with one accord
in one place.

2 And suddenly there came a sound from
heaven as of a rushing mighty wind, and
it filled all the house where they were
sitting.

3 And there appeared unto them cloven
tongues like as of fire, and it sat upon each
of them.

4 And they were all filled with the Holy
Ghost, and began to speak with other
tongues, as the Spirit gave them utterance.

Many years ago as a young denominational
pastor reading the New Testament, the Holy
Spirit enlightened me and I was convinced
that if I received the same Holy Ghost they
received I would have the same initial sign
they had—the Bible evidence—speaking with

tongues. I wasn't satisfied with anything else. Speaking with tongues is not the Holy Ghost. And the Holy Ghost is not the speaking with tongues. But they go hand in hand.

Believers Filled in Samaria

The events in the Book of Acts cover a number of years. Eight years after the day of Pentecost we see Philip carrying the gospel to the people of Samaria:

ACTS 8:5-8; 12

5 Then Philip went down to the city of Samaria, and preached Christ unto them.

6 And the people with one accord gave heed unto those things which Philip spake, hearing and seeing the miracles which he did.

7 For unclean spirits, crying with loud voice, came out of many that were possessed with them: and many taken with palsies, and that were lame, were healed.

8 And there was great joy in that city . . .

12 But when they believed Philip preaching the things concerning the kingdom of God, and the name of Jesus Christ, they were baptized, both men and women.

These scriptures helped me to see that there is an experience subsequent to salvation called receiving the Holy Ghost. I had been taught that when you are saved you have the Holy Ghost—which is true in a sense. But my denomination taught you had all the Holy Ghost there was.

Jesus said, *"Go ye into all the world, and preach the gospel to every creature. He that believeth and is baptized shall be saved; but he that believeth not shall be damned"* (Mark 16:15-16). These Samaritans believed and were baptized (Acts 8:12). Were they saved? According to Jesus they were.

There is a work of the Holy Spirit in the new birth, but that is not called receiving the Holy Ghost—that is called being born-again, receiving Eternal Life. There is an experience following salvation called receiving, or being filled with the Holy Ghost.

When the apostles at Jerusalem heard of the wonderful things God had done through Philip's ministry in Samaria, they sent Peter and John to lay hands on the new converts that they might receive the Holy Ghost.

ACTS 8:14-17
14 Now when the apostles which were at Jerusalem heard that Samaria had received the word of God, they sent unto them Peter and John:

15 Who, when they were come down,
prayed for them, that they might receive the
Holy Ghost:
16 (For as yet he was fallen upon none
of them: only they were baptized in the
name of the Lord Jesus.)
17 Then laid they their hands on them,
and they received the Holy Ghost.

Now some who object to speaking with
tongues argue that the Bible doesn't mention
the Samaritans spoke with tongues when they
received the Holy Ghost. But—it doesn't say
they didn't! Students of church history know
that the early church fathers agree they did
speak with tongues in Samaria. And it also
seems apparent from this passage that they did
speak with tongues for:

ACTS 8:18
18 And when Simon (the sorceror—see
verse 9) saw that through laying on of the
apostles' hands the Holy Ghost was given,
he offered them money,
19 Saying, Give me also this power, that
on whomsover I lay hands, he may receive
the Holy Ghost.

"When Simon saw . . ." the Word says.
You can't see the Holy Ghost. He is a Spirit
and cannot be seen with the physical eye.

6

There had to be some physical sign whereby Simon would know they had received the Holy Ghost—something which would register on Simon's senses. All evidence indicates the sign manifested was speaking in tongues.

Believers Filled in Cornelius' Household

About ten years after the day of Pentecost the Word tells us about Peter's going to Cornelius' house to carry the gospel.

ACTS 10:44-46
44 While Peter yet spake these words, the Holy Ghost fell on all them which heard the word.
45 And they of the circumcision which believed were astonished, as many as came with Peter, because that on the Gentiles also was poured out the gift of the Holy Ghost.
46 For they heard them speak with tongues, and magnify God.

Reading the entire account of this we see how an angel appeared to Cornelius and told him to send to Joppa, and to inquire in the house of a certain individual for Simon Peter, *"Who shall tell thee words, whereby thou and all thy house shall be saved."* Neither Cornelius nor his household was saved. They were Jewish proselytes. A person can't be saved without hearing the gospel. They didn't know about Jesus. So Peter preached to them. They believed while they were standing there and were born again as Peter preached. Then they received the Holy Ghost and spoke in tongues before he finished his message.

Notice that it was the speaking with tongues which convinced Peter's company that these Gentiles had received the Holy Spirit. The Jewish believers were astonished that the Holy Spirit was poured out on the Gentiles.

Believers Filled in Ephesus

Then 20 years after the day of Pentecost, Paul journeyed to Ephesus. There he met some believers and introduced to them the Person of the Holy Ghost.

ACTS 19:1-3,6
1 And it came to pass, that, while Apollos was at Corinth, Paul have passed through the upper coasts came to Ephesus: and finding certain disciples,
2 He said unto them, Have ye received the Holy Ghost since ye believed? And they said unto him, We have not so much as heard whether there be any Holy Ghost.
3 And he said unto them, Unto what then were ye baptized? And they said, Unto John's baptism.

6 And when Paul had laid his hands upon them, the Holy Ghost came on them and they spake with tongues, and prophesied.

As we see from the verses above, these believers at Ephesus had never heard about the Holy Ghost. But when Paul laid his hands on them, the Holy Ghost came upon them, and they spoke with tongues. Every one of them—without waiting, without praising, without tarrying—was filled with the Holy Ghost and spoke with other tongues as the Spirit of God gave them utterance.

Paul's Infilling of the Spirit

Paul, who laid hands on these folks, was previously known as Saul of Tarsus. The account of his experience of receiving the Holy Ghost is found in the ninth chapter of Acts.

ACTS 9:10-12, 17

10 And there was a certain disciple at Damascus, named Ananias; and to him said the Lord in a vision, Ananias. And he said, Behold I am here, Lord.

11 And the Lord said unto him, Arise, and go into the street which is called Straight, and inquire in the house of Judas for one called Saul, of Tarsus: for, behold, he prayeth,

12   And hath seen in a vision a man named Ananias coming in, and putting his hand on him, that he might receive his sight.

17   And Ananias went his way, and entered into the house; and putting his hands on him said, Brother Saul, the Lord, even Jesus, that appeared unto thee in the way as thou camest, hath sent me, that thou mightest receive thy sight, and be filled with the Holy Ghost.

Saul, later to be known as Paul, received the Holy Ghost immediately. He didn't have to tarry or wait. He received instantly.

"But it doesn't say he spoke with tongues," someone might object. It is true it doesn't say it specifically right here. But Paul himself said that he spoke with tongues. He said, *"I thank my God, I speak with tongues more than ye all"* (I Cor. 14:18). We know he didn't start talking with tongues before he received the Holy Ghost. It shouldn't be too difficult to figure out when he started. He started when he received the Holy Ghost, just as the rest of us did, for the tongues go along with it.

Speaking with tongues is an initial supernatural sign or evidence of the Holy Spirit's indwelling. It is the beginning of it all. I have found in my own life that the more I pray and worship God in tongues, the more manifestation of other gifts of the Spirit I have. The less I talk in tongues, the less manifestation I have. Speaking with tongues is the door into the rest of the spiritual gifts.

PART II

TEN REASONS WHY EVERY BELIEVER SHOULD SPEAK IN TONGUES

"And these signs shall follow them that believe . . . they shall speak with new tongues" (Mark 16:17).

The apostle Paul wrote much about the subject of speaking in other tongues. He apparently practiced what he preached for he said, *"I thank my God, I speak with tongues more than ye all"* (I Cor. 14:18). I too, thank God that I speak in tongues with regularity, and would wish for every believer this same blessing and source of power in his everyday life. The purpose of Part II of this book is to set forth major reasons why every Christian should speak in tongues, and to help believers see the blessings which can be theirs through appropriating the power of the Holy Spirit daily.

Reason 1 — Tongues the Initial Sign

ACTS 2:4

4 And they were all filled with the Holy Ghost, and began to speak with other tongues, as the Spirit gave them utterance.

The Word of God teaches that when we are filled with the Holy Ghost, we speak with other tongues as the Spirit of God gives utterance. It is the initial evidence or sign of the Baptism of the Holy Spirit. Therefore, the first reason people should speak with other tongues is—this is a supernatural evidence of the Spirit's indwelling.

In the tenth chapter of Acts we read where the Jewish brethren who came with Peter to Cornelius' house were astonished when they saw that the gift of the Holy Ghost was poured out on the Gentiles. They thought it was just for the Jews. How did these Jews know that Cornelius' household had received the gift of the Holy Ghost? *"For they heard them speak with tongues, and magnify God"* (Acts 10:46). Speaking in tongues was the supernatural sign which convinced them the Gentiles had the same gift as they.

Reason 2 — Tongues For Spiritual Edification

I CORINTHIANS 14:4

4 He that speaketh in an unknown tongue edifieth himself.

In writing to the church at Corinth, Paul encouraged them to continue the practice of speaking with other tongues in their worship of God and in their prayer lives as a means of spiritual edification. Greek language scholars tell us that we have a word in our modern vernacular which is closer to the meaning of the original than the word "edified." That word is "charge"—as used in connection with charging a battery. Therefore we could paraphrase this verse, "He that speaketh in an unknown tongue edifies, charges, builds himself up like a battery." And this wonderful, supernatural means of spiritual edification—notice that it is not mental nor physical edification—is for every one of God's children.

I CORINTHIANS 14:2

2 For he that speaketh in an unknown tongue speaketh not unto men, but unto God: for no man understandeth him; howbeit in the spirit he speaketh mysteries.

Weymouth's translation of this verse says, "He speaks divine secrets." God has given to the church a divine, supernatural means of communication with Himself.

I CORINTHIANS 14:14
14 For if I pray in an unknown tongue, my spirit prayeth, but my understanding is unfruitful.

Notice that this says, *"my spirit prayeth."* The Amplified translation reads, "my spirit, by the Holy Spirit within me, prays."

God is a Spirit. When we pray in tongues, our spirit is in direct contact with God, who is a Spirit. We are talking to Him by a divine, supernatural means.

It is amazing how people can ask in the light of these scriptures, "What is the value of speaking in tongues?" If God's Word says speaking in tongues is of value—then it is of value. If God says it edifies—then it edifies. If God says it is a supernatural means of communication with Himself—then it is a supernatural means of communication with Himself. If God says every believer should speak in tongues—then every believer should speak in tongues. Jesus did not say that just a few should speak in tongues. He said, *"And these*

signs shall follow them that believe . . . "
"Them" is plural—it means all. And one of the
signs was, ". *. . they shall speak with new
tongues . . ."* (Mark 16:17.)

Reason 3 — Tongues Remind us of The Spirit's Indwelling Presence

JOHN 14:16-17
16 And I will pray the Father, and he
shall give you another Comforter, that he
may abide with you for ever;
17 Even the Spirit of truth; whom the
world cannot receive, because it seeth him
not, neither knoweth him: but ye know
him; for he dwelleth with you, and shall be
in you.

Howard Carter, who was general supervisor
of the Assemblies of God in Great Britain for
many years, and founder of the oldest Pente-
costal Bible school in the world, pointed out
that we must not forget that speaking with
other tongues is not only the *initial* evidence
of the Holy Spirit's infilling, but is a *con-
tinual* experience for the rest of one's life.
For what purpose? To assist us in the worship
of God. Speaking in tongues is a flowing
stream which should never dry up, and will
enrich the life spiritually.

Continuing to pray and worship God in tongues helps us to be ever conscious of His indwelling presence. If I can be conscious of the indwelling presence of the Holy Ghost every day, it is bound to affect the way I live.

A minister's twelve-year-old daughter once lost her temper and was talking rudely and hatefully to her mother. A visiting evangelist overheard the scene. When the girl looked up and saw him, knowing he had witnessed her tantrum, she was embarrassed and broke into tears.

"I'm so sorry you saw me act this way and heard what I said," she cried.

"Honey," he said, "there is One greater than I am who saw you and heard you. You are a Christian, aren't you?"

"Yes."

"And filled with the Spirit?" he asked.

"Yes."

"Well then, the Holy Ghost is in you. He knows what you said, and how you acted. But if you will repent, the Lord will forgive you."

They prayed together. She repented and in a little while began to worship God in tongues.

Then he said to her, "Here is a secret that will help you curb your temper. If you will pray and worship God every day in tongues, it will help you to be conscious of the indwelling presence of the Holy Ghost. If you will remember that He is in you, you won't act that way."

Some years later the evangelist returned to preach at that church, and the pastor's daughter told him, "I have never forgotten what you said. Every day for the past few years I have prayed and worshiped God in tongues—and I have never lost my temper again."

Unfortunately, we all know people who have been filled with the Holy Ghost, yet still lose their temper and say and do things they shouldn't. This is only because they haven't been walking in the Spirit as they should. It is so easy, when we are not conscious of His presence, to become irritated and frustrated. But if we will take time to fellowship with Him, we can be ever conscious of His indwelling presence.

Reason 4 — Praying in Tongues is Praying in Line With God's Perfect Will

ROMANS 8:26-27

26 Likewise the Spirit also helpeth our infirmities: for we know not what we should pray for as we ought: but the Spirit itself maketh intercession for us with groanings which cannot be uttered.

27 And he that searcheth the hearts knoweth what is the mind of the Spirit, because he maketh intercession for the saints according to the will of God.

Speaking in tongues keeps selfishness out of our prayers. A prayer out of one's own mind and thinking has the possibility of being unscriptural. It may be selfish. Too often our prayers are like the old farmer's who prayed, "God bless me, my wife, my son John, his wife —us four and no more."

In the scripture quoted above Paul didn't say we didn't know how to pray—for we do. We pray to the Father in the name of the Lord Jesus Christ, which is the correct way to pray. But just because I know how to pray doesn't mean I know what to pray for as I ought. Paul said, ". . . *We know not what we should pray for as we ought: but the Spirit itself (himself) maketh intercession for us with groanings which cannot be uttered."*

P. C. Nelson, a scholar of the Greek, said that the Greek literally reads here, "The Holy Ghost maketh intercession for us in groanings that cannot be uttered in articulate speech." Articulate speech means our regular kind of speech. He went on to point out how the Greek stresses that this not only includes groanings escaping our lips in prayer, but also praying in other tongues. This agrees with what Paul said in I Corinthians 14:14, *"For if I pray in an unknown tongue, my spirit prayeth . . ."* Or, as the Amplified translates, "My spirit (by the Holy Spirit within me) prays."

When you pray in tongues—it is your spirit praying, by the Holy Spirit within you. The Holy Spirit within you gives the utterance— and you speak it out of your spirit. You do the talking. He gives the utterance. By this method the Holy Spirit helps you pray according to the will of God, as things should be prayed for.

This isn't something the Holy Ghost does apart from us. Those groanings come from inside us and escape our lips. The Holy Ghost isn't going to do our praying for us. He is sent to dwell in us as a Helper and an Intercessor. He isn't responsible for our prayer lives — He is sent to help us pray.

Praying with other tongues is praying as the Spirit gives utterance. It is Spirit-directed praying. It eliminates the possibility of selfishness in our prayers.

Many times when people have prayed out of their own minds, they received things that were actually not the will of God and were not best. If God's people insist on having things a certain way, even if it isn't best for them, or is not God's perfect will, He will often permit it. God did not want Israel to have a king, but they kept insisting that they wanted one. So He permitted them to have one. But it was not His perfect will.

Reason 5 — Praying in Tongues Stimulates Faith

JUDE 20

20 But ye, beloved, building up yourselves on your most holy faith, praying in the Holy Ghost.

Praying in tongues stimulates faith and helps us learn to trust God more fully. If the Holy Spirit supernaturally directs the words I speak, faith must be exercised to speak with tongues. For I don't know what the next word will be — I am trusting God for it. And trusting God in one line will help me to trust Him in another.

As a young Baptist minister, I pastored a community church, and stayed in the home of a Methodist couple. The wife was a fine dear woman, who loved the Lord. But she had an ulcerated stomach, which doctors feared would lead to cancer. Her husband made good money, but he had spent everything he had on medical bills. I knew God could and would heal her, but somehow I was never able to lift her faith up to that point. She ate only soft foods and milk and had difficulty keeping that on her stomach. But one day a wonderful thing happened! She received the infilling of the Holy Spirit. When I came in she was eating foods she'd never been able to eat.

"I received not only the Baptism of the Holy Ghost and spoke with other tongues," she told me, "but I received my healing too. I'm perfectly well." And she was.

I've seen this happen many times. What is the connection? We know that receiving the Baptism of the Holy Ghost does not heal us. However, speaking with tongues helps us to learn how to trust God more fully. Speaking in tongues helps us to believe God for other things because it stimulates our faith.

Reason 6 — Speaking in Tongues, A Means Of Keeping Free From Worldly Contamination

I CORINTHIANS 14:28
28 But if there be no interpreter, let him keep silence in the church; and let him speak to himself, and to God.

The sixth reason every Christian should speak in tongues is that this is a means of keeping free from the contamination of the ungodly and the profane, and all the vulgar talk around us on the job or out in public.

Notice from the scripture above that we can speak with tongues to ourselves. Paul said that in the church service, *"If any man speak in an unknown tongue, let it be by two, or at the most by three, and that by course; and let one interpret. But if there be no interpreter, let him keep silence in the church; and let him speak to himself, and to God"* (I Cor. 14:27-28).

If we can speak to ourselves and to God in a church service, we can also do it on the job. It won't disturb anyone. In the barber shop, for instance, when men tell risque jokes, I just sit there and speak to myself and to God in tongues. Riding the train, bus, or airplane—we can speak to ourselves and to God. On the job—we can speak to ourselves and to God. Talking in tongues to yourself and to God will be a means of keeping free from contamination.

Reason 7 — Praying in Tongues Enables Us to Pray For the Unknown

Praying in tongues provides a way to pray for things for which no one thinks to pray, or is even aware. We already know that the Holy Spirit helps us to pray for what we know not how to pray as we ought. But in addition, the Holy Spirit—who knows everything—can pray through us for things about which our natural minds know nothing.

An English missionary to Africa was home on furlough speaking at a missionary conference when a woman asked him if he kept a diary. He replied that he did. And she began to relate to him, "Two years ago I was awakened in the night with a burden to pray. I got out of bed and was talking in tongues before I got down on my knees. For an hour I prayed in tongues—and it seemed as if I were wrestling. When I finished praying I had a vision. I saw you in a little grass hut, surrounded by natives. You were sick. Then you died. I saw the natives pull the sheet over your head and walk sadly outside the hut. Suddenly you came out of the hut and stood in their midst, and all the natives rejoiced."

The missionary then asked her if she kept a diary and requested she bring it that afternoon. Comparing diaries, and making allowances for time differences in England and Africa, they discovered the time of the woman's prayer burden exactly coincided with the time when the missionary was sick with a deadly fever. His partner was away, and he was alone with the natives. Things happened just as she saw them—the missionary died, the natives saw him die and pulled a sheet over his head—then he rose up suddenly well! Because of the Spirit of God!

In 1956 when my wife and I were in California, I was awakened suddenly in the night. It was as if someone laid his hand on me. I sat bolt upright in bed, my heart beating rapidly.

"Lord," I cried, "what is the matter? I know something is wrong somewhere. Holy Spirit in me, You know everything. You are everywhere as well as within me. Whatever this is, You give me utterance."

I prayed in tongues for an hour and then began to laugh and sing in tongues. (When praying this way, always continue praying until you have a note of praise. Then you will know that whatever it is you are praying about, is settled.) I knew what I had been praying for had come to pass. I had the answer, so I went back to sleep.

I dreamed that I saw my youngest brother become extremely ill in Louisiana. I saw an ambulance with lights flashing take him to the hospital. In the dream, I stood in the corridor outside his hospital room door. The door was shut. Then the doctor came out that door, pulled it shut behind him, shook my hand and said, "He is dead."

"No, doctor, he is not dead," I replied.

"What do you mean, he is not dead?"

"The Lord told me he would live and not die."

At that the doctor became angry and said, "Come with me and I will show you that he is dead. I have pronounced too many people dead not to know when someone is dead." He took me by the arm and led me into my brother's room. He walked over to the bed and jerked the sheet back. When he did, my brother's eyes opened. The doctor saw that he was breathing. He began to stutter, "You knew something I didn't know. He is alive, isn't he?"

In the dream I saw my brother rise up from the bed, well. That was what I had been praying about.

Three months later we came home to Texas. My brother came by to see me and said, "I nearly died while you were gone." I told him that I knew he'd had an attack during the night while staying in a motel in Louisiana, and had been rushed to the hospital. He thought someone had told me about it, but they had not. I told him about my burden of prayer followed by the dream. "That's exactly how it happened! They told me that for about 40 minutes at the hospital the doctor thought I was gone."

Praying in the spirit provides a way for things to be prayed for that we wouldn't know anything about in the natural. The Holy Ghost, however, knows everything.

Reason 8 — Praying in Tongues Gives Spiritual Refreshing

ISAIAH 28:11-12

11 For with stammering lips and another tongue will he speak to this people.

12 To whom he said, This is the rest wherewith ye may cause the weary to rest; and this is the refreshing: yet they would not hear.

What is the rest, the refreshing, the above scripture refers to? Speaking in other tongues!

Sometimes the doctor recommends a rest cure, but I know the best one in the world. Often when you take a vacation, you have to come home and rest before going back to work. But isn't it wonderful that we can take this "rest cure" every day? *"This is the rest . . . this is the refreshing . . ."* We need this spiritual refreshing in these days of turmoil, perplexity, and anxiety.

Reason 9 — Tongues For Giving Thanks

I CORINTHIANS 14:15-17

15 What is it then? I will pray with the spirit, and I will pray with the understanding also: I will sing with the spirit, and I will sing with the understanding also.

16 Else when thou shalt bless with the spirit, how shall he that occupieth the room of the unlearned say Amen at thy giving of thanks, seeing he understandeth not what thou sayest?

17 For thou verily givest thanks well, but the other is not edified.

When Paul said, "He that occupieth the room of the unlearned . . .", in verse 16, he was referring to those who are unlearned in spiritual things.

If you invited me to dinner and said, "Please give thanks;" and if I prayed in tongues you wouldn't know what I said. You wouldn't be edified. Therefore, Paul said it would be better to pray with my understanding there. If I did pray in tongues, I should interpret it so you would know what was said.

But notice that Paul says praying in tongues provides the most perfect way to pray and to give thanks, for he said, *"Thou givest thanks well."* (Verse 17.)

In the presence of people who are unlearned, however, Paul said to pray with your understanding also so that they can be edified; they will understand what you say.

Reason 10 — Speaking in Tongues Brings the Tongue Under Subjection

JAMES 3:8
8 But the tongue can no man tame; it is an unruly evil, full of deadly poison.

Yielding the tongue to the Holy Spirit to speak with other tongues is a giant step toward fully yielding all of our members to God. For if we can yield this most unruly member, we can yield any member.

The Public Side of Tongues

In conclusion I want to point out that, while we have dealt primarily with tongues in the individual believer's private life, it is also true there is a public side to tongues.

First, when people receive the Holy Ghost publicly they speak with other tongues as the Spirit gives utterance.

Secondly, the church is edified by speaking with other tongues in public assembly with interpretation. Paul plainly stated that to prophesy is to speak unto men *"to edification, and exhortation, and comfort"* (I Cor. 14:3). But he said, *"Greater is he that prophesieth than he that speaketh with tongues, except he interpret"* (I Cor. 14:5).

Paul is saying that tongues with interpretation is equivalent to prophecy—i.e., if the utterance in tongues is interpreted so that the church can understand what is said, then the one prophesying is not greater.

To illustrate, two nickels equal one dime. However, the two nickels are not a ten-cent piece. Prophecy is the dime, the ten-cent piece. Naturally, it would be better to have the dime (prophecy) than to have the nickel (an utterance in tongues). But, if interpretation (another nickel) went along with it, then the two would be equivalent to the dime.

Let me say here that prophesying is not preaching. If prophesying were preaching, then you wouldn't have to make any preparation to preach. But you have to study and prepare to preach. Paul said, *"Study to shew thyself approved unto God . . ."* (II Tim. 2:15). You don't have to study to speak with tongues, or to interpret. You don't have to study to prophesy. These come by inspiration of the Spirit. Of course, when one is preaching under the inspiration of the Spirit, and suddenly he says things he never thought of, that is inspiration and is an element of prophecy.

Tongues with interpretation edifies the church. When used in line with the Word of God, speaking with tongues with interpretation convinces the unbeliever of the reality of the presence of God, and often causes him to turn to God and be saved.

Jesus said, *"And these signs shall follow them that believe; In my name shall they cast out devils"* (Mark 16:17). That can be private or public. *"They shall lay hands on the sick, and they shall recover"* (Verse 18). That can be private or public. Another sign is, *"They shall speak with new tongues"* (Verse 17). This too, is both private and public.

Of course, we don't want prolonged praying in tongues in the service because unless there is an interpretation, folks don't know what is said and are not edified. It is all right to pray in the altar service as long as you want, for you go there to be edified. If people in the service are lifting their hands and praying, it is all right to pray in tongues. I stand on the platform and pray that way every night. But when the congregation ceases praying, I cease praying. The congregation wouldn't be edified if I went on and on.

We do need to know how to use what we have to the greatest advantage.